CROSSES 2

Decorative Patterns

Marcus Clemons

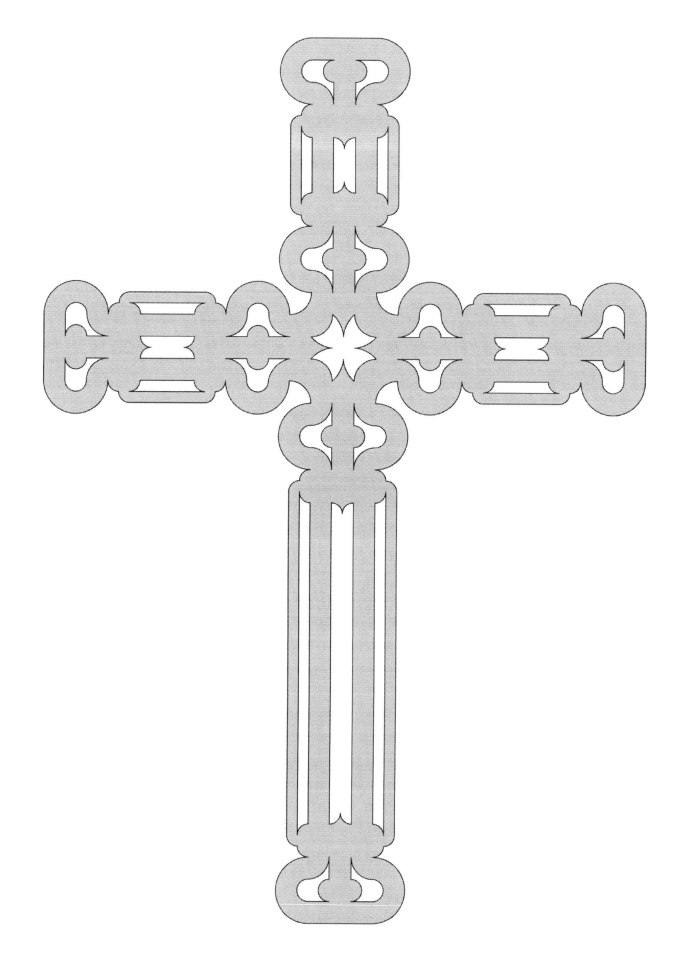

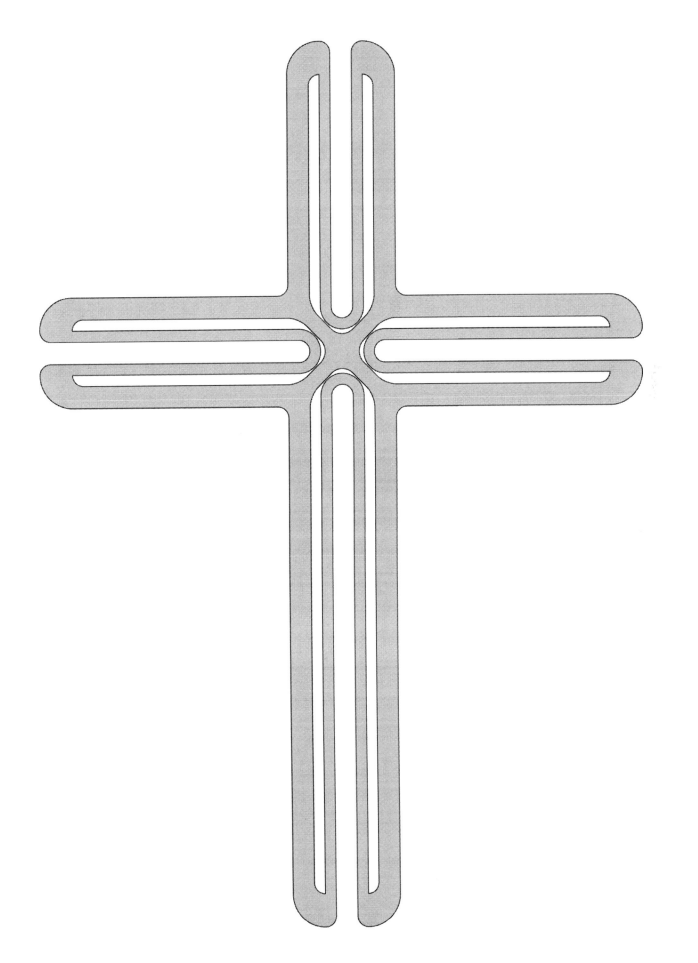

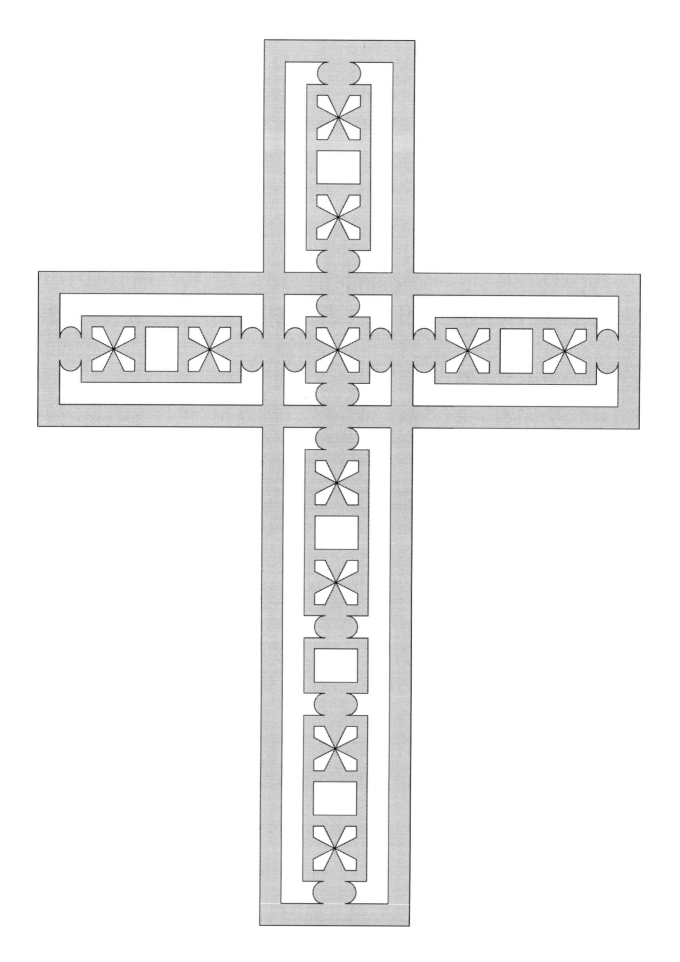

Crosses: Decorative Patterns

Crosses: Decorative Patterns provides a collection of 130 full page patterns for the creative soul, suitable for scroll saw and other artistic endeavors.

Crosses: Decorative Patterns
140 pages
ISBN-13: 978-1512224320
ISBN-10: 1512224324

Rosettes: Scroll Saw Patterns

Rosettes: Scroll Saw Patterns series, is designed to be a quick reference for crafting projects, giving the user a large library of over1300 rosette patterns from which to work. Each style of rosette is cropped to eight sizes per page, allowing for simple mix-and-match design techniques.

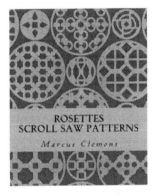

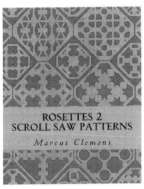

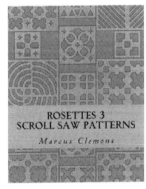

ROSETTES: Scroll Saw Patterns
172 pages
ISBN-13: 978-1500299873
ISBN-10: 1500299871

ROSETTES 2: Scroll Saw Patterns
172 pages
ISBN-13: 978-1500624088
ISBN-10: 150062408X

ROSETTES 3: Scroll Saw Patterns
172 pages
ISBN-13: 978-1500843755
ISBN-10: 150084375X

Bookmarks: 400 Patterns

Bookmarks: 400 Patterns presents a collection of four styles of bookmark, each with 100 patterns, suitable for use across multiple mediums.

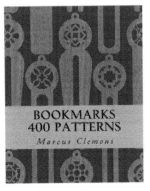

Bookmarks: 400 Patterns
98 pages
ISBN-13: 978-1507546796
ISBN-10: 1507546793

Made in the USA
San Bernardino, CA
04 December 2018